I Know The Plans
I Have For You

I Know The Plans
I Have For You

Lydia Van Ek

To order additional copies of this book, contact:
Xlibris Corporation
1-888-795-4274
www.Xlibris.com
Orders@Xlibris.com
66192

CONTENTS

1. GENESIS 13

2. STRUGGLES 19

3. A GOOD REPORT 30

4. HIS STORY 35

5. FIRST DAY OF THE WEEK 37

6. ROBYN 45

7. REVELATION 53

DEDICATION:

I wish to dedicate this book to my parents who brought their large family from Holland all the way to Sooke, British Columbia, Canada in 1952.

I acknowledge, however, that it is my Heavenly Father who gave me this book. He quickened my spirit. I am complete in Him. He opened my ears and the eyes of my understanding and asked me to put my life's experiences in writing. I chose to trust and obey.

This is my story, worth telling because of its' universal application. My journey has been marked with struggles, questions, longings and so many rich blessings. The journey is not unique but what is special is that writing this book has been an exciting privilege. The tow-headed little Dutch girl who once came close to elective mutism has found her voice. Her life has become a message.

The message is for everyone who will listen, for everyone who is tired, hungry and thirsty who has more questions than answers. You will read of others as well whose lives have been transformed by yielding to the Master's touch.

It is my prayer that what I have written will be an encouragement and an inspiration especially for my family but for all of my readers. God bless you.

"Everyone needs compassion, a Love that's never failing
Let mercy fall on me. Everyone needs forgiveness, the kindness of a
Savior
THE HOPE OF NATIONS

Refrain:
Savior, He can move the mountains, my God is Mighty to save Yes,
He's Mighty to save. Forever, Author of salvation
He rose and conquered the grave. Jesus conquered the grave.

So take me as you find me, all my fears and failures. Fill my life again.
Everything I believe in, I give my life to follow. I surrender.

Shine a light and let the whole world see. For the glory of the Risen
King
JESUS"

Hillsongs (Australia)

DISCLAIMER

In writing my life story I cannot help but write about those persons who have greatly influenced my life, particularly by way of familial relationship. I do not wish to discredit any individual or to malign anyone's character. For this reason no names, apart from biblical characters and Jesus, THE NAME ABOVE ALL NAMES, are included. I no longer fear man because I know that man is not my enemy. God's grace, mercy and forgiveness are free and readily available for one and all.

At the heart of my message is the firm belief that:

> **"We are not wrestling with flesh and blood (contending only with physical opponents), but against the despotisms, against the powers, against (the master spirits who are) the world rulers of this present darkness, against the spirit forces of wickedness in the heavenly (supernatural) sphere." Ephesians 6:12 (Amplified)**

CHAPTER 1

GENESIS

I was born in Leiden, South Holland, in 1949, the youngest of 10 children with 6 brothers and 3 sisters. Our father worked hard to provide for his family and because of post WW II economic hardships he decided to take the opportunity given and brought us all to Canada in February 1952. Our family was sponsored by the Wilford family in Sooke, British Columbia at the Woodside Farm. The Wilfords had sponsored other families before us including some of our relatives. Upon our arrival, some of our cousins, aunts and uncles were already in the farm house so we were accommodated just across the road at Moss Cottage. There was no indoor plumbing but an outhouse. Only one bedroom inside and being the youngest I got to sleep where my parents slept. My brothers slept in little outer cabins on the property. Moss Cottage was surrounded by broome bushes so thick that you could throw yourself down against them and not be hurt at all. Dad had built a huge see-saw and swing for us in the yard. My playmates and I would make necklaces by placing the bright yellow petals of the broome bush one at a time on the long green stems. We would pick and eat mint leaves. Mmmm. But watch out for those stinging nettles. Ouch! Moss Cottage, by the way, has been re-located and is currently on site at the Sooke Museum. The Woodside Farm is recognized as an historic site as well.

In October of 1953 I contacted polio. I became delirious with high fever. We were living in the farmhouse at that time. I have been told that I saw my dad's woollen socks walking around the room but he was not in them. Over the next several days I would collapse, my left leg would give out as I was walked along. My mom took me to the doctor and poliomyelitis was the diagnosis, 10 days before my fourth birthday. My family was put in quarantine for a period of time because there was a polio epidemic in Europe concurrent. At that young age I was taken from my family and deposited into a strange new world of doctors, nurses, surgeries, isolation, ether masks, frightening emotions, foreign language, new foods, new expectations, the list goes on. After consultation with the orthopaedic surgeon I would be taken to the hospital from home and put in isolation for several days so that no one else could come in contact with the infectious disease with which I had been diagnosed. No one could explain to me why I was being isolated because of the language barrier. It felt like torture to me. Post surgery was equally traumatic for me and I remember it well. I was wheeled, bed and all, in front of the nurses' station in the hall so they could keep an eye on me. That was not so bad. What I could not understand was why my head was lower than my feet. They did not want my blood flow to go to the area where I had been operated on but to me I was being punished again. I must have done something wrong but I did not know what it was. I felt so very alone. (4-year old tow-headed dutch girl's perspective)

I was admitted to the Royal Jubilee Hospital for surgery and then discharged to the Queen Alexandra Solarium for a time of physiotherapy and recouperation. I would be allowed to go home for a few months before the process would be repeated for assessment and more necessary surgery. In the meantime my parents moved from Sooke to Port Alberni and back to Sooke. They were in Port Alberni for a couple of years. Once when they came to visit me at the hospital they could not find me because I had been moved to the solarium. My parents thought I had died. Can you imagine how hard that must have been on them? They could only visit me once in two weeks while I was at the solarium because of the distance from home and all of their other responsibilities. Eventually I hated to see my parents come because I knew they were only going to leave. Dad would have to pry my fingers off of mom's wrists every time so they return home. My siblings were not allowed to visit.

Everything I needed to know for life and living I was learning before I was old enough to go to school. I learned to fight for my life as I struggled against those green-suited doctors until I succumbed to the ether mask which was held over my nose and mouth. Nothing could be explained to be because I did not understand the language nor did I have a clue what was going on in my little body. I felt abandoned, I knew isolation, learned to be afraid of man but I also gradually came to understand that there are many kind people in the world. The doctors and nurses would take me with them on coffee breaks and offer me sugar cubes, sometimes doughnuts. I had a special police escort when travel was necessary between the solarium at Brentwood Bay and the Royal Jubilee Hospital. These experiences away from home and family taught me self-reliance and resourcefulness. The years between 1953 and 1957 show 5 separate admissions and discharges on hospital and solarium records. This 4-year period of my life represents a significant part of my beginning and greatly impacts the person I am today.

Oh, how I loved growing up on the farm. I have such fond memories of Sooke and the Woodside Farm especially. I loved to roam the property which is on the Pacific Ocean playing at the seashore collecting bits of salt-water-washed-up-colored glass. Next to the beach there was a swamp and the bigger boys would build rafts using materials like logs, seaweed, kelp, ropes, whatever they could find. What fun we would have trying to navigate the swamp and stay dry. The gooey mud underneath was not so pleasant if your raft fell apart. The swamp would actually freeze in the winter welcoming skaters.

Every season offered its pleasures on the farm. I remember cutting figures out of catalogues—men, women, children and babies. We would outfit them and have hours of fun. I enjoyed climbing trees, riding on the backs of gentle cows and swinging back and forth high above in the hayloft of the barn. Wonderful childhood memories of kick-the-can and baseball too. Trees were plentiful and in good variety on Woodside Farm. I could climb as high as I dared in the borrowed strength of those tall Douglas Firs. I remember sitting on top of the Hazelnut tree. It was like being in a bird's nest. We did not have a television at that time but from this vantage point we could look down into the living room of neighbours and there was a tiny blue box with some moving images we could not quite make out what they were, however, we were watching television.

Blackberries grew in succulent abundance and within relative easy access on the farm. Mom would make vanilla custard and bessensap oh, so very yummy. In fact, everything in the kitchen was made from scratch. Sometimes Mom baked for her Ladies Aid Society meetings. I used to complain because those special treats were not for us at home. We would have inhaled all of that in one minute or less. She baked fresh bread twice a week and we would spread butter on the warm bread and sprinkle sugar on it. Mmmm good. Dad grew a huge vegetable garden. He prepared the soil with his plough, rotor tiller and harrow pulled behind the tractor. He would prepare other people's land so they could garden. Dad's full time employment was at the Sooke Saw Mill. He was a very resourceful and hardworking man always doing whatever he could to provide for his family. We sold vegetables at a roadside stand. We snacked on whole cucumbers like they were apples. I remember watching my dad catching chickens and chopping their heads off. Kind of fun to see a chicken running around with its' head chopped off. We kept rabbits as well—for eating. My sister and I did manage one year to put one or two of the rabbits in the Sooke Fall Fair but we, that is our rabbits, were never prize-winners.

We had a dog named Spotty who followed me wherever I went which was normally okay except for this one day when I happened to be coming home from the beach across the fields and had to go through the orchard where the cows were. Apple trees were plentiful on the 40-acre farm. Spotty started to bark at the cows making me nervous. I thought I would be smart and climb an apple tree to get away from the cows but the lower branches barely cleared the cows' backs. Spotty just stayed at the tree's base barking incessantly in spite of my orders for him to go home. I thought I would bombard the cows with apples to shoo them away but I only prolonged my stay in the tree. In time the cows lost interest, Spotty lost his voice and I was able to climb down and go home.

Dad built a house for his family across from the farm on the West Coast Road when I was a young girl. He built it in his spare time and I believe he did most, if not all of the work himself. I remember helping him with some of the work. I would bring him tea and a sandwich from home across the field and through the wire fence. I loved to be with my dad. I would pick up the scrap bits of lumber, nail them together and create. Dad was forming the cement foundation at that time and my 'creations' became part of the filler. Dad worked so hard doing whatever he could to provide for his family and at the end of the day he still enjoyed just being with his wife and children. He never accumulated much wealth in this world and yet he was a generous man. I remember him doling out dimes, nickels and pennies on a weekly basis. No one was left out.

I completed my first and second grades of elementary school in Port Alberni and then we were back in Sooke living in the beautiful big farmhouse. I loved life on the farm as I have said before. I was so happy to be home and out of the hospital for good, or so I hoped and prayed. I overheard a doctor telling my mom that I should have another operation when I was 12. I couldn't sleep for the last couple of weeks as my twelfth birthday approached. Mom asked what was wrong. I told her what I had overheard and thankfully, she assured me that my fears would not be realized.

Sooke Elementary School was a favorite place of mine. I played tetherball at school and became the tetherball champion. I enjoyed brownies, learned to ride a bike on the farm, swam at the Sooke River Potholes and went to church regularly. I remember writing in my grade 3 journal that I wanted to be a missionary when I grew up. I loved to sing and I joined the community choir. My sister and I innocently embarrassed our parents when with pride we sang a duet on stage for a Sooke community event. We were beautifully dressed for the occasion and both parents attended. They were horrified by the song which had been chosen for us. With lusty voices we burst forth "Old Flip drank, drank, drank drank too much. The boss came home and asked him such and such. Is Flip my man not here? Is Flip my man not there? Well then, he's on his journey to America." No more of that choir for my sister and I. We often sang duets at church and that was good. My sister and I had dishes to do at home and if we started to argue about who would wash and who would dry, mom would interject and tell us to sing instead of argue and sing we did. Another lesson mom was firm on "Thou shalt not gossip." We learned to do our chores and to treat each other with respect. Our parents were good providers, left a legacy of a good work ethic and paved the way for their children to live a life of faith in God.

Celebrations were fun at our house. Speculaas and gevulde koek were always favorite eating delights and zoute drop of course. The birth of a new grandchild was cause to celebrate with beschuit met muisjes and hagelslag. Dad would make oliebollen by the barrel each New Year's Eve and we would play games like touwtje trekken and sjoelen. I must say that dad did some cooking too. His expertise, however, apart from the oliebollen, was relegated to outside of the kitchen because of lingering odors produced by those fried kippers and herring.

While reading through the Bible I have noticed parallel experiences in the lives of several great men and women of faith. I mention some now in terms of their beginnings—Moses, David and Joseph.

Moses had to be hidden when he was born because of the oppression of the Israelites by the Egyptians. He was taken from his mother and become the son of the Pharaoh's daughter. (Exodus 2)

(I Samuel 16:7) The Lord told Samuel to go to Jesse and anoint one of his sons to be the next king of Israel. (**"The Lord sees not as man sees; for man looks on the outward appearance but the Lord looks at the heart."**) Seven sons passed before Samuel but none were chosen. David was overlooked by his family. considered insignificant. vs 11 **"There remaineth yet the youngest, and behold, he keepeth the sheep."** vs 12 **"Arise, anoint him: for this is he."**

Joseph too, had a rough start in life. His brothers hated him because he was the favourite child of their father.

My parents had been in the habit of attending church in Holland 3 times on a Sunday. Things were different in Sooke. There was only one service in the morning at the Knox Presbyterian Church. Mom and dad could not afford to drive to Victoria to attend the Christian Reformed church as much as they would like to. The Plymouth Brethren started a work in the afternoon on Sundays and some years later Sunday evenings as well at the Milne's Landing Gospel Chapel. My parents were invited and we all started attending. We had no vehicle at the time and the whole family walked the 5 or 6 miles both ways for 2 services on Sunday. I am told that I was carried. I enjoyed the services at the Gospel Chapel very much and soon my sister and I had another venue for our duets. The missionaries explained that if the children would do a Bible correspondence course and memorize chapters of scripture and they could attend a week of summer Bible at no cost. I did the work with pleasure and ease. In the summer of my ninth year I attended my first free camp at Maple Bay, Camp Imadene, Faithful to The Faith, and there I heard the salvation message and asked Jesus to come into my heart. I prayed and told Him that I believed that He died on the cross to pay the penalty for my sins. I received forgiveness and cleansing that day in June 1959. I went back to camp several years running and it was always the highlight of my summer. My sister and I would come home with plenty of choruses to keep us singing while doing dishes.

If asked to sing for you today I am confident that my sister and I would sing:

My Lord has garments so wondrous fine, And myrrh their texture fills;
Its fragrance reached to this heart of mine With joy my being thrills.

Refrain
Out of the ivory palaces, Into a world of woe,
Only His great eternal love Made my Savior go.

His life had also its sorrows sore, For aloes had a part;
And when I think of the cross He bore, My eyes with teardrops start.

In garments glorious He will come, To open wide the door;
And I shall enter my heav'nly home, To dwell forevermore.

CHAPTER II

STRUGGLES

This chapter in my life is the most difficult for me to write. Knowing it is imperative to my message and with a desire to obey, I press on.

> *I Corinthians 10:13 "No trial has overtaken you that is not belonging to human experience. But God is faithful to His Word and to His compassionate nature and He can be trusted not to let you be tried and assayed beyond your ability and strength and power to endure. He will always provide the way out to a landing place that you may be capable and strong and powerful to bear up under it patiently."*
> *(Amplified)*

God in His wisdom provided the idyllic setting of Sooke for my landing place. Children possess an innate ability to block out unpleasant memories. They are quick to forgive and forget. My growing up years until graduation from high school presented a wonderful time of healing, recovery and growth in my new relationship with Jesus. I was a good girl leading a sheltered life and I had no clue that there were some pretty serious struggles ahead. In my grade 11 year I got a job at the local pharmacy as a clerk. The pharmacist actually offered me the job one day. He was a wonderful man. He let me drive his Volkswagen 'bug' to make deliveries. I was so proud. Even though I had only thirty minutes for lunch I would drive home, wolf down a sandwich, take the car behind the house and wash it before returning to work. Once in a while the pharmacist, my boss, allowed me to work right beside him at the counter filling prescriptions. He said that anyone could count pills. There was no one else in the store at those times. One day he handed me an envelope. Inside the envelope was a note and a cheque for $200. The note read "This is a small token of the measure of faith that my wife and I have in you and your ability to succeed." Those words were wonderful although somewhat overwhelming for me.

At the end of grade 12 I was chosen to give the valedictory address as my sister had been 2 years before me. Now what? No one in my family had gone on to further education. All of my brothers had enlisted in the Canadian Armed Forces (army, navy and air force). My 2 older sisters were married and had families of their own. My sister had her first child by this time. I had thought about going to University but my parents did not like the idea and tried to discourage me. My parents wanted to leave Sooke. Mom did not drive, had finished raising her family but I hated the thought of leaving Sooke.

My university student number begins with the year I graduated high school. I travelled from Sooke to Victoria the first year and then my parents moved to Victoria. My first year was so difficult I failed most of my courses. I was ill prepared for all the studying and the disciplined lifestyle necessary for success. I did not really know what I was doing or what I wanted to do at that point. I was not happy living at my parents home. They had bought a tiny house with one bedroom. Rabbits had been kept where I was to sleep. Ugghh! Mom made sure the space was clean but there was no privacy, it was wide open to the kitchen. One early morning I will not forget was when dad stood over my bed and sleeping head conversing with a stranger about his plans for the space I was occupying. How embarrassing! It did not take long for dad to convert the garage into a workshop and add on a bedroom for me at the back behind the bathroom/laundry room. As much as I appreciated my new bedroom on Haultain Street, I can still remember crying out to God in despair asking Him to please reveal Himself to me. I remember feeling so very alone. I was failing at university, at life and living in general. I believed it was time for me to get out on my own.

The years that followed leaving my parents' home quickly filled with difficult lessons on life and how to live it. I was faithfully attending Victoria Gospel Chapel but even there I felt so alone. I stopped going because when people saw me they wouldn't ask how I was doing. Instead, they would say, "How is your sister? We haven't seen her in a long while." She had always been the pretty one, the popular one. I felt invisible, uncared for. I went looking for friends in the wrong places. When I complained to my sister about being lonely (at that time I babysat for her often) she hooked me up with an acquaintance of her husband who took me for a drive, walked me into the woods, gave me my first taste of liquor, talked to me about sex and had intercourse with me. I remember his incredulity at my ignorance and my virginity. I never saw him again. I will interject here that I recall the day I started menstruating and how frightened I was. I did not know what was happening to me and was afraid I might be dying. What I did know was that I was losing an awful lot of blood. My sister routinely insisted that she and her boyfriend were the last off the bus to make the walk home together at the end of the school day. I was supposed to lead the way but on that particular day there was no way I would let them or anyone else see whatever it was that was happening to me. I can be stubborn too. I refused to move once I had stepped off the bus, until all others had passed in front. Once we were home, my sister asked for an explanation of my behaviour. She comforted, advised and told me that she had not been educated about this event in her life either. Mom eventually had said to her "Oh, don't worry, even Queen Elizabeth has this." My sister thought that she and the queen were the only 2 people in the world with this horrible affliction.

The illicit relationship leading to rape, mentioned above, was the first of several in the ensuing years. For several months I had a room in a house where the kitchen and bathroom were shared. In search of friendship I accepted an invitation, from a girl who lived in one of the other rooms, to go to a bar—another new experience for me. A new friend followed me home and chose to stay with me—for a week. We got along very well and he asked for my hand in marriage. I laughed at this and told him he hardly knew me. I knew our relationship was not right because I was troubled in my spirit and I had not told him about my relationship with Jesus Christ. Being in the Navy, he had to go back on board ship and I never saw him again. Something he told me I will always remember. "You are naïve, intelligent and stubborn."

When I was not attending classes full time at the University I was working full time as a civil servant. I worked for the Department of Veterans' Affairs, the Ministry of Transportation & Highways, Revenue Canada and the Institute of Ocean Sciences. The difficult lessons in my life were ongoing during these years complete with more illicit relationships and an increasing awareness of conflicting emotions within.

In my second year of university, on the education program, I needed to complete my practicum. I asked to do my practicum at Sooke Elementary. The principal, who had been my fifth grade teacher while I attended there, took me down the hall and said "I am putting you with a teacher I am confident you will get along very well with." My teaching practicum was a wonderful, unforgettable and most successful experience. The teacher chosen for me was a new Christian and had been praying that God would send another Christian to join her on staff. She told me that I was the answer to her prayer. We became life long friends during those weeks. She invited me to her home and to her church and so after several months of not attending church I felt welcomed and loved.

I took a summer job in Golden, BC as a desk clerk receptionist at a hotel. My girlfriend and I lived in a tent when we first arrived. I was friendly with the clients. A nice man invited me to go for a ride with him on his motorcycle. I did and enjoyed the ride. He asked where I was staying and I told him. Later he found our campsite when my girlfriend was on her shift at the hotel, came into my tent and raped me. I believe that I did not even realize that I had been violated because I told no one about this event for decades.

When I was back in Victoria I started attending Bible studies in homes and there I met the person who later became my husband. We had many good times together. We shared a love of the out of doors, a true appreciation of nature and we liked to be together. He was so at ease with groups of people—the opposite of me. From time to time I remember feeling puzzled by his behaviour, especially if we were alone, and wondering what he was thinking or feeling but I felt confident that there would be nothing going on that love would not be able to fix and I certainly had an abundance of love to offer him. He was not able to express his feelings or to let me know what he was thinking about. Unfortunately, in this relationship too, there were no boundaries set regarding intimacy because I had not yet fully understood who I was in Christ and had little, if any, sense of self.

Before I proceed I feel this is the appropriate place to say that **I believe that there is a spirit behind every form of disobedience** and as already mentioned in my disclaimer at the book's start I know that man is not my enemy. This is important to repeat here:

> *"We are not wrestling with flesh and blood (contending only with physical opponents), but against the despotisms, against the powers, against (the master spirits who are) the world rulers of this present darkness, against the spirit forces of wickedness in the heavenly (supernatural) sphere." Ephesians 6:12 (Amplified)*

In the spring of 1969 I received my teaching certificate but I did not have a position in the Victoria School District so I continued my work as a civil servant. My husband-to-be was now attending the same church and had asked Jesus into his heart. We continued to struggle in our relationship, received counselling and tried to abstain from sexual relations but were not successful. In the early seventies I accepted a teaching position in Prince George and taught grade one for 2 years. My husband-to-be came to visit during the spring of my second year of teaching and proposed marriage. I accepted. We were married August 14, 1976. On our honeymoon the physical abuse began. The first 3 months of our marriage were so horrible I knew they had to get better. I was told to be quiet. He only needed me. We attended church faithfully, even held Bible studies in our home. Night after night I would try to comfort, calm and help him any way I could only to be beaten and abused in the wee hours of the morning. In the daytime I enjoyed keeping house—cooking, baking, trying new recipes and cleaning. I was going to university part time as well. I had one year to complete the classes needed for my bachelor of education degree on a 4 yr program. Everything would be' just so' for when my husband got home from work, the table set and food all prepared. I would not know if he would want to eat right away. He might prefer to go out first and eat later. I would never know what, if anything, might set him off, or be a trigger for his anger. I remember the time when he overturned our meal, dishes and all, in a split second.

By the tenth month of our marriage I knew the silence must be broken if I was going to survive. I spoke to our pastor who suggested a counselling service. We went for several visits 2 weeks apart. I prayed and hoped that the counsellor would be able to help us. After our third or fourth visit this particular counsellor told us that we were doing fine and he saw no reason for us to continue. I was disappointed. We left the building and my husband drove through the city like a crazy man. He nearly caused an accident with his swerving. At one point, in his anger and frustration, he grabbed a fistful of my hair and pounded my head against the side window, actually cracking the window. Not a word was spoken. No counsellor can help a person who is not able to admit that they have a problem and would like some help. At that point in my life I was not strong enough to speak up, I expected the counsellor to see things that were being kept hidden. When we arrived home, as soon as my husband stepped out, I immediately locked both doors of the Datsun pick-up and just stayed put. I stayed put for several hours until I thought I might be able to safely get out and over to a neighbour's. As soon as both of my feet were on the gravel driveway, there he was knocking me down to the ground. I got up and he knocked me down again. This went on until I reached the doorstep around the corner at which point he punched me in the face and actually drew blood. All of the other abuse up to this point in our marriage, although physical, had resulted in bruising and could be covered by clothing. This was different. The sight of blood spewing from my eyebrow startled my husband. What had he done? He quickly got a dishtowel and took me to the emergency room at the hospital. After some stitching the attendant asked me if I would tell him who had done this to me and if it was my husband. I told him that it was. He told my husband to call a friend and have them come and pick me up. My husband called our friend who had been my maid of honour. I stayed at her and her husband's house for several days.

"I have A Maker, He formed my heart
Before even time began, My life was in His hands

Chorus:
He knows my name
He knows my every thought
He sees each tear that falls
And hears me when I call

I have a father, He calls me His own
He'll never leave me, No matter where I go."

Genesis 37:5-8;28

"One night Joseph had a dream, and when he told his brothers about it, they hated him more than ever. 'Listen to this dream," he said. "We were out in the field, tying up bundles of grain. Suddenly my bundle stood up, and your bundles all gathered around and bowed low before mine!" His brothers responded, "So you think you will be our king, do you? Do you actually think you will reign over us?" And they hated him all the more because of his dreams and the way he talked about them."

"When the Ishmaelites, who were Midianite traders, came by, Joseph's brothers pulled him out of the cistern and sold him to them for twenty pieces of silver. And the traders took him to Egypt."

Psalm 105: 17-19 "Joseph, who was sold as a slave. They bruised his feet with fetters and placed his neck in an iron collar. Until the time came to fulfill his dreams, the LORD tested Joseph's character."

My husband had begun to apprentice as an electrician in Victoria and because of the state of the economy at that time his employer went bankrupt. My husband managed to get an apprenticeship with another firm but a few months later that firm also declared bankruptcy. After sending resumes and requests for employment to several Vancouver Island cities he was hired in Campbell River in the summer of 1978. I gave 2 week's notice to the Institute of Ocean Sciences and joined my husband in Campbell River at the end of June.

Perhaps a fresh start would be good for us. I hoped and prayed that would be the case. On that first holiday weekend we joined the Baptist church group for their Sunday school picnic at beautiful Rebecca Spit on Quadra Island. We settled in to life in CR and were both working, attending church, bible study and prayer meetings. It wasn't too long before I had to call on the pastor for help, however, to deal with my troubled and abusive spouse. In October we left our rented apartment having purchased a lovely 2-bedroom rancher in a quiet cul-de-sac. I did not know at the time that I was pregnant. Our first daughter arrived in July 1979. The physical abuse continued and I began to realize that more drastic measures had to be taken if the cycle of abuse was going to be arrested. I went to see a lawyer, threatened to take him to court, however, the abuse continued. I knew if I did not follow through on my threat I could be in serious danger. One night when some of my family were visiting from out of town, I took our daughter, in the middle of the night, and escaped to a friend's house to stay for a while—another separation. My husband did seem remorseful during the time of separation. Also, I remember him using some of that time to fix things around the house, something he did not usually do. Several months after we were reconciled I had a miscarriage. Some more months passed and I was pregnant with our second child, still the abuse had not stopped. Our second daughter arrived in March 1981. My husband wanted to go into business for himself. He had been studying, earned his 'C' ticket and had become a qualified journeyman electrician. I became pregnant with our third child. In April 1983 we sold our house, my husband launched his electrical contracting business and I went into hospital to deliver daughter number 3 while friends moved us into our new home. Our lives had become very busy. Our second daughter was in preschool and the teachers noticed behavioural challenges with her. An Educational Psychologist visited our home, asked questions and observed her. Her comment was that my child's behaviour was not abnormal rather, it was normal in an abnormal environment. Unfortunately, our personal/relational issues, at home, were receiving very little, if any, of the attention they so desperately needed.

In the summer of 1985 I noticed that I was having difficulty coping in a general kind of way that I could not really understand. I seemed to be falling apart and that frightened me. I called my husband and asked him to come home and help me. He told me that he would come home in a while. Several hours passed. I was getting worse and called a neighbour who was very concerned about me, taking me to the emergency room because at that point I could not stop crying. The doctor said I could not go home without an appointment at Mental Health so I made one. I was very surprised to find myself sitting across the desk from a lady who had been a year or 2 ahead of me in school in Sooke. We had a talk and it was not long before she said to me "You know what you have to do." My husband's sister and family were coming to visit for the upcoming July 1st holiday weekend and it was then, with the help of a girlfriend, that I packed up my 3 young daughters, some clothing and bedding and we left Campbell River for Victoria. This was the start of a 2-year separation. Our oldest daughter started first grade in the fall and her sister went to a Montessori kindergarten. She was still troubled and needed the help of a psychologist and psychiatrist as referred by either her teacher or family physician. My second daughter had a fear of men and would not go near any doctor for treatment. The recommendation of the psychiatrist was a period of 're-training' in a local institution. I could not fathom being separated from my daughter for any length of time so I did not register her for this program. We had a psychologist visit and observe in our home (referral from Montessori principal) resulting in a report that was quite satisfying to me. He was very complementary on my interactions with my three daughters and my abilities as their mother. During these 2 years I made a deliberate effort to uphold a good image of my daughter's father for their sakes and to keep as much of our family's routines the same as was possible.

When school was out in 1987 we went home to Campbell River. Along with helping in the electrical contracting business I did some substitute teaching at the Campbell River Christian School. I was offered a full time position there but after some consideration, I declined because our children were still quite young. In 1989 my dad passed away. Since this reconciliation the physical abuse had stopped. Gradually I began to realize, however, that the abuse was still a part of our relationship and had only changed forms (emotional, verbal and financial). I kept myself busy running the household, driving our girls to their many after-school events and commitments. I did the necessary paperwork to incorporate the electrical contracting business and became the Secretary. In 1993 I accepted a position as learning assistance teacher at the Campbell River Christian School where I taught for 2 years. In the spring of 1995 when the new school was being built I was told that my contract would not be renewed for the next year. The reason I was given was "Due to concern for your state of well being and the condition of your family it has been decided not to renew your contract." I did not understand. I recalled my principal complimenting me on the work that I did with the students who had difficulties learning, even asking me to explain what it was that I was doing that was so effective. After some thought I had replied to him that I could relate to these students and find a way to get across to them the information they needed to know because, like them, I was not a stranger to struggles. I was also able to uncover and build upon the strengths which all of my students possessed. I was working with a private counsellor at that time who became very upset that I was not angry about the non-renewal of my teaching contract but, when I fought the decision, I was fired.

Depression had set in for me and things were not improving at home. I felt that it would be best for my husband and I to separate but that the girls and I should not be the ones to leave this time. Without getting upset, I asked him to leave and he did. For approximately 6 months he lived about 15 miles south of town. I allowed him to come and go from the property as he sheds full of electrical equipment and supplies off the driveway. What peace I enjoyed for a time. One morning he came upstairs into the kitchen saying there was something he would like to talk with me about. "What would you think if I bought a piece of property?" he asked. I was impressed that he would ask my opinion and I also knew that this was something that would mean a great deal to him. "Go for it!" I said. What I did not know, nor did he tell me until sometime later, was the fact that he had already bought a piece of property and that the piece of property just happened to be across the road from our current address. I had stopped doing the bookkeeping during the time of this separation. I started a tutoring business out of my home. I also began to provide part-time care for a special needs infant who was born in Campbell River in 1996. The Receiver General wanted to audit the electrical business with respect to GST. Because I had been involved in the family business since it started, I volunteered to go over all of the invoices and statements to record the GST. This took approximately 40 hours. I put my results in a big brown envelope and drove to Victoria having made an appointment with Revenue Canada. The auditor was impressed and told me that I had saved the company over ten thousand dollars by doing the work I had done and avoiding the audit.

My husband's father passed away suddenly in May 1997 and only 3 months later, in August, his mother passed away. I felt that he must be devastated and of course this was an extremely difficult time for him. I am only being honest when I say that I also hoped that our girls and I would now occupy a more important place in his heart. In the light of these events I invited my husband to move back home. Our girls and I helped with the move back across the street. It took only 3 weeks for me to ask myself "What have I done?" "Why did I think things would be any different?" His behaviour on one particular day made it very clear to me that things were not going to change. I felt so desperate because I had promised that I would not ask him to leave nor would I leave again. I lost the will to live. Then I remembered.

Isaiah 58:6 "Is not this the fast that I have chosen? To loose the bands of wickedness, To undo the heavy burdens, And to let the oppressed go free, And that ye break every yoke?"

I made a decision that day in August 1997 to take God at His word. I fasted and prayed for 3 weeks. I got no clear answer right away. After another week I fasted for another week or so. Then I heard whisper of God's voice speaking to my spirit, telling me to come to Victoria and look after my mother. I did not leave until the end of December but from that day I had calm assurance and renewed purpose. With resolve I told my husband of my plans sometime in October.

The book of Psalms is a passionate display of the many emotions of David, "the man after God's own heart." Acts 13:22 David is no stranger to struggles.

Psalm 13:2-4 "How long shall I take counsel in my soul, Having sorrow in my heart daily? How long shall mine enemy be exalted over me? Consider and hear me, O LORD my God: Lighten mine eyes, lest I sleep the sleep of death; Lest mine enemy say, I have prevailed against him;"

Psalm 18:1-6 "I will love thee, O LORD, my strength, The LORD is my rock, and my fortress, and my deliverer; My God, my strength, in whom I will trust; My buckler, and the horn of my salvation, and my high tower. I will call upon the LORD, who is worthy to be praised: So shall I be saved from mine enemies. The sorrows of death compassed me, And the floods of ungodly men made me afraid. The sorrows of hell compassed me about: The snares of death prevented me. In my distress I called upon the LORD, And cried unto my God: He heard my voice out of his temple, And my cry came before him, even into his ears."

Psalm 22:9-22 "But thou art he that took me out of the womb: Thou didst make me hope when I was upon my mother's breasts. I was cast upon thee from the womb: Thou art my God from my mother's belly. Be not far from me; for trouble is near; For there is none to help. Many bulls have compassed me: Strong bulls of Bashan have beset me round. They gaped upon me with their mouths, As a ravening and a roaring lion. I am poured out like water, And all my bones are out of joint: My heart is like wax; It is melted in the midst of my bowels. My strength is dried up like a potsherd; And my tongue cleaveth to my jaws; And thou hast brought me into the dust of death. For dogs have compassed me: The assembly of the wicked have enclosed me: They pierced my hands and my feet. I may tell all my bones: They look and stare upon me. They part my garments among them, And cast lots upon my vesture. But be not thou far from me, O LORD: O my strength, haste thee to help me. Deliver my soul from the sword; My darling from the power of the dog. Save me from the lion's mouth: For thou hast heard me from the horns of the unicorns."

CHAPTER III

A GOOD REPORT

Looking over Proverbs 31, I can say with confidence that I have looked well to the ways of my household, opened my mouth with wisdom, on my tongue is the law of kindness, I am clothed with strength and honour, I have sought to reach forth my hands to the needy and my children have called me blessed, they praise me and thank me for the many fine things I do and have done for them.

Proverbs 31:30 "Favour is deceitful, and beauty is vain: But a woman that feareth the LORD, she shall be praised."

The following is some of the feedback I received at the end of a 10-month lay-counselling program I participated in several years ago.

"Your courage and compassion for others and your dedication to becoming a wonderful counsellor will always be an inspiration to me."

"Never forget your quiet courage Lydia, I know I never will. Your strength has always been obvious and will always serve you."

"From day one you have inspired me to be me. Your determination and inspiration for all out of life you can get is awesome. You are a great gift and you will be a great gift to your clients."

"Thank you so much for your caring heart and friendship."

"Thank you for the 'gift' of yourself in our group. You have really inspired me by your gentleness, wisdom and courage. Thank you for touching my life."

"I've decided to take up a whole page for you because maybe if I write more you will begin to realize how much you mean to me. From the moment I met you

I have felt connected to you. You are such a beautiful person. Your calm and loving energy makes me want to sit on your lap!"

David had to be fetched from the fields where he was tending sheep. In those fields David had fought and killed both a lion and a bear while protecting the sheep. He tossed aside a king's heavy armour, defeating Goliath with his slingshot and 5 smooth stones. Samuel had come to his father Jesse's house by God's instruction to anoint the future king. David grew to become "a man after God's own heart." Acts 13:22. He won many military victories as Israel's king.

I Samuel 18:14 "And David behaved himself wisely in all his ways; and the LORD was with him."

Things seemed to go from bad to worse for Joseph upon his arrival in Egypt. He found favour with the Pharaoh but, for refusing to sleep with Potiphar's wife, Joseph was put in prison. There he interpreted the dreams of the chief butler and baker. They forgot him upon their release from prison. When the Pharaoh needed help with the interpretation of his dreams, however, the butler remembered that Joseph had interpreted his dream. Joseph told Pharaoh Genesis 41:16 "It is not in me: God shall give Pharaoh an answer of peace."

Joseph went on to become the governor over the land during the time of famine and was able to be a blessing to his family. The LORD was with him and everything he did was made to prosper. Joseph told his family . . . .

> **Genesis 45:7 "God sent me before you to preserve you a posterity in the earth, and to save your lives by a great deliverance."**

Moses, the deliverer, led the children of Israel out of Egypt. He later acted as an intercessor for the people. The Israelites got tired of waiting for Moses' return and has erected golden images to worship, kindling God's anger.

> **Exodus 32:11-14 "LORD, why doth thy wrath wax hot against thy people, which thou hast brought forth out of the land of Egypt with great power, and with a mighty hand? Wherefore should the Egyptians speak, and say, For mischief did he bring them out, to slay them in the mountains, and to consume them from the face of the earth? Turn from thy fierce wrath, and repent of this evil against thy people. Remember Abraham, Isaac, and Israel, thy**

servants, to whom thou swearest by thine own self, and sadist unto them, I will multiply your seed as the stars of heaven, and all this land that I have spoken of will I give unto your seed, and they shall inherit it forever. And the LORD repented of the evil which he thought to do unto his people."

Exodus 33:17, 20, 22 "And the LORD said unto Moses, I will do this thing also that thou hast spoken: for thou hast found grace in my sight, and I know thee by name . . . And he said, Thou canst not see my face; for there shall no man see me, and live . . . And it shall come to pass, while my glory passeth by, that I will put thee in a cliff of the rock, and will cover thee with my hand while I pass by."

Hebrews 11:22-40 "It was by faith that Joseph, when he was about to die, said confidently that the people of Israel would leave Egypt. He even commanded them to take his bones with them when they left. It was by faith that Moses' parents hid him for three months when he was born. They saw that God had given them an unusual child, and they were not afraid to disobey the king's command. It was by faith that Moses, when he grew up, refused to be called the son of Pharaoh's daughter. He chose to share the oppression of God's people instead of enjoying the fleeting pleasures of sin. He thought it was better to suffer for the sake of Christ than to own the treasures of Egypt, for he was looking ahead to his great reward. It was by faith that Moses left the land of Egypt, not fearing the king's anger. He kept right on going because he kept his eyes on the one who is invisible. It was by faith that Moses commanded the people of Israel to keep the Passover and to sprinkle blood on the doorposts so that the angel of death would not kill their firstborn sons. It was by faith that the people of Israel went right through the Red Sea as though they were on dry ground. But when the Egyptians tried to follow, they were all drowned. It was by faith that the people of Israel marched around Jericho for seven days, and the walls came crashing down. It was by faith that Rahab the prostitute was not destroyed with the people in her city who refused to obey God. For she had given a friendly welcome to the spies. How much more do I need to say? It would take too long to recount the stories of the faith of Gideon, Barak, Samson, Jephthah, David, Samuel, and all the prophets. By faith these people overthrew kingdoms, ruled with justice, and received what God had promised them. They shut the mouths of lions, quenched the flames of fire, and escaped death by the edge of the sword. Their weakness was turned to strength. They became strong in battle and put whole armies to flight. Women received their loved ones back again from death. But others were tortured, refusing to turn from God in order to be set free. They placed their hope in a better life after the resurrection. Some were jeered at, and their backs were cut open with whips. Others were chained in prisons. Some died by stoning, some were sawed in half, and others were killed with the sword. Some went about wearing skins of sheep and goats, destitute and oppressed and mistreated. They were too good for this world, wandering over deserts and mountains, hiding in caves and holes in the ground. All these people earned a good reputation because of their faith, yet none of them received all that God had promised. For God had something better in mind for us, so that they would not reach perfection without us."

Hebrews 12:1-2 "Therefore, since we are surrounded by such a huge crowd of witnesses to the life of faith, let us strip off every weight that slows us down, especially the sin that so easily trips us up. And let us run with endurance the race God has set before us. We do this by keeping our eyes on Jesus, the champion who initiates and perfects our faith. Because of the joy awaiting him, he endured the cross, disregarding its shame. Now he is seated in the place of honor beside God's throne."

You are BEAUTIFUL beyond description.
Too MARVELLOUS for words.
Too WONDERFUL for comprehension.
Like nothing ever seen or heard.
Who can grasp your INFINITE wisdom?
Who can fathom the depths of your LOVE?
You are BEAUTIFUL beyond description.
MAJESTY enthroned above.

And I stand, I stand in awe of you.
I stand, I stand in awe of you.
HOLY GOD to whom all praise is due.
I stand in awe of you.

Above all powers above all kings
Above all nature and all created things
Above all wisdom and all the ways of man
You were here before the world began

Above all kingdoms above all thrones
Above all wonders the world has ever known
Above all wealth and treasure of the earth
There's no way to measure what You're worth

Crucified laid behind a stone
You lived to die rejected and alone
Like a rose trampled on the ground
You took the fall and thought of me
Above all

CHAPTER IV

HIS STORY

The birth of Jesus Christ, the messianic king, was prophesied in Isaiah.

Isaiah 9:2; 6-7 "The people that walked in darkness have seen a great light: They that dwell in the land of the shadow of death, upon them hath the light shined. For unto us a child is born, unto us a Son is given: And the government shall be upon his shoulder: And his name shall be called Wonderful, Counsellor, The mighty God, The everlasting Father, The Prince of Peace. Of the increase of his government and peace there shall be no end, Upon the throne of David, and upon his kingdom, To order it, and to establish it with judgment and with justice From henceforth even forever. The zeal of the LORD of hosts will perform this."

Further in Isaiah's prophetic scriptures we read more of Jesus' life story. All came to pass exactly as written.

Isaiah 53 "Who hath believed our report? And to whom is the arm of the LORD revealed? For he shall grow up before him as a tender plant, And as a root out of a dry ground: He hath no form nor comeliness; And when we shall see him, there is no beauty that we should desire him. He is despised and rejected of men; A man of sorrows, and acquainted with grief: And we hid as it were our faces from him; He was despised, and we esteemed him not. Surely he hath borne our griefs, And carried our sorrows: Yet we did esteem him stricken, Smitten of God, and afflicted. But he was wounded for our transgressions, He was bruised for our iniquities: The chastisement of our peace was upon him; And with his stripes we are healed. All we like sheep have gone astray; We have turned everyone to his own way; And the LORD hath laid on him the iniquity of us all. He was oppressed, and he was afflicted, Yet he opened not his mouth: He is brought as a lamb to the slaughter, And as a sheep before her shearers is dumb, So he openeth not his mouth. He was taken from prison and from judgment: And who shall declare his generation? For he was cut off out of the land of the living: For the transgression of my people was he stricken. And he made his grave with the wicked, And with the rich in his death; Because he had done no violence, Neither was any deceit in his mouth. Yet it pleased the LORD to bruise him; he hath put him to grief: When thou shalt make his soul an offering for sin, He shall see his seed, he shall prolong his days, And the pleasure of the LORD shall prosper in his hand. He shall see of the travail of his soul, and shall be satisfied: By his knowledge shall my righteous servant justify many; For he shall bear their iniquities. Therefore will I divide him a portion with the great, And he shall divide the spoil with the strong; Because he hath poured out his soul unto death: And he was numbered with the transgressors; And he bare the sin of many, And made intercession for the transgressors.

Man of Sorrows! What a name
For the Son of God, who came
Ruined sinners to reclaim.
Hallelujah! What a Savior!

Bearing shame and scoffing rude,
In my place condemned He stood;
Sealed my pardon with His blood.
Hallelujah! What a Savior!

Guilty, vile, and helpless we;
Spotless Lamb of God was He;
"Full atonement!" can it be?
Hallelujah! What a Savior!

Lifted up was He to die;
"It is finished!" was His cry;
Now in Heav'n exalted high.
Hallelujah! What a Savior!

When He comes, our glorious King,
All His ransomed home to bring,
Then anew His song we'll sing:
Hallelujah! What a Savior!

CHAPTER V

FIRST DAY OF THE WEEK

John 20:1 "The first day of the week cometh Mary Magdalene early, when it was yet dark, unto the sepulchre, . . ."

2009 marks the sixtieth year of my life and Sunday, the first day of the week, has always been the most important day of each week for me. There have been relatively few Sundays in my life where I have not attended church. Most Sundays have been the happiest day of my week but it can be a very sad day.

My parents were members of the Dutch Christian Reformed Church in Holland and faithfully attended as much as they could after bringing the family to Sooke. They believed in **Proverbs 22:6 "Train up a child in the way he should go: And when he is old, he will not depart from it."** As a young child I was taught to pray before and after each meal as well as before going to sleep at night. I remember the bedtime prayer:

> Ik ga slapen Ik ben moe
> 'k Sluit mijn beiden oogjes toe
> Here houd ook deze nacht
> Over mij getrow de wacht.

I still remember the 'pepermuntjes' that were passed at a certain time in the service each Sunday morning. Singing, especially in church, has been a huge legacy passed on by my parents. The dutch had a unique way of singing hymns. One Christmas song which gives me goose bumps to this day if I hear it is:

> *Ere zij God, Ere zij God*
> *In den hoge, In den hoge, In den hoge*
> *Vrede op aarde, vrede op aarde*
> *In de mensen, een welbehagen*

Ere zij God in den hoge
Ere zij God in den hoge
Vrede op aarde, vrede op aarde,
In de mensen, een welbehagen
In de mensen, een welbehagen,
Een welbehagen.

(translation) Glory to God in the highest. Peace on earth. Goodwill towards men.

The Christian Reformed Church had a choir which mom and dad joined. I was invited to join as a teenager. We would drive from Sooke one evening during the week to rehearse, a very special time for me. I will never forget performing the Hallelujah Chorus with that choir. Several years later I sang the Hallelujah Chorus with the University Chorus, one of 400 voices in Christ Church Cathedral and an unforgettable event for me. As I mentioned in Chapter I, my parents could not keep up the travel to the Christian Reformed Church in Victoria so we attended the Knox Presbyterian Church in Sooke. In my earlier writing I mentioned also that my family and I attended the Milne's Landing Gospel Chapel in Sooke and later the Victoria Gospel Chapel where I was baptized as a believer in Jesus Christ. **Matthew 28:19 "Go ye therefore and teach all nations, baptizing them in the name of the Father, and of the Son, and of the Holy Ghost:"** In my late teen years and early twenties I began to experience some difficult times even in my church life. Some of the painful emotions of my early childhood began to re-surface. I felt as if I were invisible, had no friends and for a while I stopped going to church. **Hebrews 10:25 "Not forsaking the assembling of ourselves together, as the manner of some is; but exhorting one another: and so much the more, as ye see the day approaching."** I am grateful to this day for my lifelong friend who encouraged me at that difficult time in my life and invited me to come to church with her. She not only shared her classroom with me for my teaching practicum but she welcomed me into her home. We continue to have many good times together. I was attending the Evangelical Free Church and there I was married.

Almost without exception Sundays would find myself and my family at the Campbell River Baptist Church. For the most part **Psalm 122:1 "I was glad when they said unto me, Let us go into the house of the LORD."** was my experience in Campbell River. I looked forward to Sundays and would enjoy preparing our children for Sunday school and worship time. We attended Bible study and prayer meetings as well. I remember many visits with the pastor(s) and counselling sessions seeking help for our troubled marriage. I realized over the years that you can go to church regularly but stay the same in your spiritual condition if you do not want to change. Both parties must want the help.

In the early 1990's I found myself depressed and not understanding my depression because, after all, how could a Christian be depressed? I went to my doctor for help. One other thing I did, on advice of a good friend, was to attend a Twelve Step Program for Christians that was being held at the Church of The Way every Monday evening. I went every Monday night for 5 years. I did not know anyone there that first night but joining that program was one of the best decisions of my life. One Monday evening when I arrived the pastor was the only one outside the church. He was cancelling because of the snowy weather conditions but I showed up just the same. That meeting was like a lifeline for me, I was learning so much about myself and finding that others had experiences similar to mine.

In February 1996 the Campbell River Baptist Church joined in prayer for a child who had been born to a family, members of the church, and flown to Vancouver BC Childrens' Hospital for treatment in the neonatal unit. We first met this beautiful special needs child, named Robyn, in the nursery at church. She later came into our home at 5 months of age where we began to provide part time care and respite. One of my daughters provided care for her in her home in Campbell River before we moved to Victoria.

I remember one Sunday in particular when I was feeling desperate about our situation at home. I was crying out to God during the service, praying quietly and pleading with Him for an answer. I did not know what to do or where to turn for help. My answer came almost immediately in the next song we were instructed to sing. It was **Be Still And Know That I Am God** I knew that was my answer. God had spoken to me and calmed my heart. I needed to be quiet and stop running to man for answers that they could not give me, just trust God. It was not long after this time that I was led by the Holy Spirit to move to Victoria to take care of my mother.

When my daughters and I moved to Victoria we took some time to look for a church where we would feel comfortable. Over a period of months my daughters and I found places of fellowship we were satisfied with. My mother lived with us from January to October 1998 (in October mom moved to Abbotsford to live in Ebenezer Care home where one of her sons was the administrator for the duration of her stay) and she loved to come to come along to church. I remember mom singing loudly, lagging a little, when she recognized a familiar hymn like, "What A Friend We Have In Jesus". It was a little embarrassing but I was not about to ask her to be quiet.

We provided respite for Robyn 2 weeks out of every month. Robyn's mom would bring her down from Campbell River and pick her up again. Robyn loved to come to church also, enjoying the music especially. My daughters preferred Saanich Baptist whereas I enjoyed Lambrick Park, a community church. I had been invited to a ladies study for single moms. The group leader is a counsellor. I enjoyed this group Bible study. I was receiving counselling, attending home study groups and trying to achieve a sense of balance and calm in my life since leaving Campbell River.

Wanting closure, in the year 2000 I filed for divorce. In July of 2000 my mother passed away. I miss her every day and I think of her often. I believe that she is always with me really because she is in my heart. I flew to the East Coast to visit my sister for 2 weeks. We had a wonderful time together and talked of living together one day. My sister came to Victoria to live with me in July of 2001. My sister was not comfortable attending that church which I had the habit of attending. I was still driving my daughters to the church that they wanted to attend and sometimes we would try a different one. My sister would simply walk out the door. For her sake I agreed to try and find a church where we would both feel comfortable. I was so relieved on the Sunday after the service at Oaklands Chapel when my sister announced that she approved of the service. I asked if we could please stop looking now. I thought that things would be fine for us at Oaklands. Soon, however, I somehow fell into an old pattern of 'invisibility'. No one would talk to me, or so it seemed and I complained to my sister. My sister offered to stay home with Robyn on a Sunday evening so I could take in the Bible study. I tried really hard to become part of the group. I studied the workbook so I could contribute intelligently to the discussion. I remember one of the elders, the study group leader, asking me one Sunday evening "How is your leg?" I was incredulous, not to mention heartbroken, that all I was to this person was a 'leg'. Oh well, I should have known better than to place my hope in man. Once again, I was finding out that church can be a very lonely place. Bringing Robyn to church was becoming increasingly difficult as she was not always comfortable in her wheelchair and often had to be removed from the sanctuary. She enjoyed the worship service and the singing particularly but most often I would end up in the foyer during the message time because of her behaviour. Sometimes when the order of service had been rearranged we would miss the worship service altogether and I would wonder why I had bothered to leave home. Robyn and I would go for long drives on those days.

From 1999 until 2003 I was living in Esquimalt and owned a 3-bedroom condominium. I thought 2 of my daughters would be living with me plus Robyn but my 2 older daughters got a place on their own before I moved. I rented a room to a friend who introduced me to a ministry called DWJD or Do What Jesus Did. I attended meetings every other Saturday for several months and was greatly blessed by this ministry in the area of deliverance.

With my daughters I had also been to Colwood Pentecostal a number of times and there I had met a young man who was passionate about worship. I admired his obvious love for Jesus. My sister and I were not getting along. For some reason Sundays were extra strained in our relationship. She confessed to me one day that she did not like her behaviour towards me, especially as Sundays approached. She said she did not really understand what was going on. I remember early one Saturday morning when my young friend, passionate about Jesus, buzzed our condo. He had been at a coffee shop witnessing to a lady for several hours and he wanted to bring her to my place to ask for prayer. I had already invited him to the DWJD meeting coming up at 10 am later that morning. We had a powerful time of prayer. I felt bad that he would miss the meeting but he felt that he had already been there. My sister was very troubled during this time. I was able to explain to my sister, in a very calm manner, that I believed she too, needed deliverance.

While living in Esquimalt I frequently passed by the Victoria Bridge Club. I had learned the basics of the game while visiting with in-laws, holiday times, over the years when our children were small. At home I was re-acquainting myself with the game, on-line, and was now considering entering the club premises. I walked in off the street one day, introduced myself and asked if I might be able to play bridge there. I received a warm welcome. Over the weeks and months that followed I found myself more and more drawn to this pastime. It seemed to provide some things that were lacking in my life. Other players seemed interested in getting to know me and would actually talk to me. I was learning this challenging game quickly, there is always more to learn, I could hardly wait until the next chance to meet for a game. In Victoria you can play bridge every day of the week, more than once a day, if you wish and can afford to. My sister would sometimes provide care for Robyn so I could attend a special bridge event such as a tournament, for example. I remember the Christmas in Esquimalt that was so very difficult between my sister and I before I sold my condo and we moved to View Royal. Holidays can be such painful times for those who are hurting. I remember Thanksgiving weekends and the thoughtfulness of my second daughter. She would make sure I was okay because the rest of the family would have been invited to a special turkey dinner and I was the only one not there. In October 2003, on the Thanksgiving weekend, my former husband was remarried. He arranged for all of our children, including our 11-month old granddaughter, to join him in Alberta for the wedding celebration. It was an extremely painful Thanksgiving weekend for me. I played in a bridge tournament and did my best to take care of myself. Two months later. During the following Christmas season, my sister made a trip back East over New Year's and out of determination to take care of myself, emotionally, I planned a potluck and bridge party in our home during the time she was away. A good time was had by all. Some weeks later, however, I woke up in the middle of the night with the realization that I had become more passionate about the game of bridge than I was about my relationship with Jesus. I confessed and told Him I was willing to give up the game because I did not trust myself to keep things under control. I thought it should be all or nothing. I renewed my commitment to Jesus Christ and His right to have first place in my life. He assured me that I did not need to give up the game. All He wanted from me was my confession. Jesus wants to be the number one 'need-meeter' in my life. He wants me to come to Him with my brokenness, in my loneliness and despair. I renewed my trust in Jesus as my Friend, Advocate, Financial Advisor, Healer and Counsellor.

Yes, I had been to church most every Sunday of my life but it is not about attending. It is not about membership. It is not even about the ordinances of baptism and communion. **I Corinthians 11:25 "For as often as ye eat this bread, and drink this cup, ye do shew the Lord's death till he come."** It is not about religion at all. It is all about relationship, relationship with the person of JESUS CHRIST. **Hebrews 13:8 "Jesus Christ the same yesterday, and today, and forever."**

Not only was my sister unhappy with the church(es) I had been attending, she was unhappy with the place I was living in Esquimalt. I was caring for Robyn and she had begun to care for a special needs child as well. Unlike Robyn, he was not wheelchair bound but completely mobile and my sister felt that he needed a single family dwelling with a yard, not my condominium. My sister was also having thoughts about going back East and being reconciled to her husband. Once again, my life was in turmoil. I remember driving around the Victoria waterfront by the hour while Robyn was in school, singing, praying and crying out to God on behalf of my sister and myself. We had come to another crossroad in our lives and some tough decisions had to be made. After some weeks I encouraged my sister to stay and look after the child. She was doing a wonderful job with him. I was willing to give up my condo and we would look for a place for the 4 of us. We rented a 2-bedroom rancher in View Royal, April, 2003.

Some weeks after the prayer meeting in my Esquimalt condo, my worship leader friend and I met for coffee. He invited me to the first meeting of the Redeemed Christian Church of God in Victoria, Victory Chapel. He told me about a pastor and his family who had responded to God's call and come to Victoria, all the way from Nigeria. I attended the first service on August 10, 2005. I did not regularly attend Victory Chapel until sometime during their second year. What I was hearing at Victory Chapel was reminiscent of the unadulterated teachings of God's Word that I had heard as a young child in Sooke at Milne's Landing Gospel Chapel and later at Victoria Gospel Chapel. One Sunday I became so frustrated at Oaklands. I felt that I had gone for nothing but disappointment and I was loading up Robyn into her lift-equipped van for another drive when I remembered that Victory Chapel was just down the hill. In all likelihood the service would still be ongoing. The two of us entered the doors and were greeted by the pastor "You look beautiful" he said. That was music to my ears. I have been attending regularly ever since that day. This pastor emanates love to one and all. Much, much more than attending has been taking place in my life and heart at Victory Chapel, which I will share in the last chapter. Here I am no longer invisible. I have found where I belong, a place where church, the body of Christ, is endeavouring to be a biblical example of what church should be.

The church's one foundation is Jesus Christ her Lord;
She is his new creation by water and the Word.
From heaven he came and sought her to be his holy bride;
With his own blood he bought her, and for her life he died.

Elect from every nation, yet one o'er all the earth;
Her charter of salvation, one Lord, one faith, one birth;
One holy name she blesses, partakes one holy food,
And to one hope she presses with every grace endued.

Though with a scornful wonder we see her sore oppressed,
By scisms rent asunder, by heresies distressed,
Yet saints their watch are keeping; their cry goes up, "How long?"
And soon the night of weeping shall be the morn of song.

Mid toil and tribulation, and tumult of her war,
She waits the consummation of peace forevermore;
Till, with the vision glorious, her longing eyes are blest,
And the great church victorious shall be the church at rest.

Yet she on earth hath union with God the Three in One,
And mystic sweet communion with those whose rest is won.
O happy ones and holy! Lord, give us grace that we
Like them, the meek and lowly, on high may dwell with thee.

CHAPTER VI

ROBYN

I Corinthians 1:27-31 "for God selected (deliberately chose) what in the world is foolish to put the wise to shame, and what the world calls weak to put the strong to shame. And God also selected (deliberately chose) what in the world is lowborn and insignificant and branded and treated with contempt, even the things that are nothing, that He might depose and bring to nothing the things that are, So that no mortal man should (have pretence for glorying and) boast in the presence of God. But it is from Him that you have your life in Christ Jesus, Whom God made our Wisdom from God, (revealed to us a knowledge of the divine plan of salvation previously hidden, manifesting itself as) our Righteousness (thus making us upright and putting us in right standing with God), and our Consecration (making us pure and holy), and our Redemption (providing our ransom from eternal penalty for sin). So then, as it is written, Let him who boasts and proudly rejoices and glories, boast and proudly rejoice and glory in the Lord."

Being careful not to wet the keyboard with my tears as I write this chapter, I will share some words given to me at the time of Robyn's passing this earth's scene. All who had the privilege of working with her quickly loved her and were greatly impacted by her life.

December 9, 2008 "I was a care-worker with Robyn for the last 2 years. Robyn was a happy, strong and courageous soul. She inspired me immensely. It was delightful to see her smile, her enjoyment of music, and her happy playing. I shall miss her very much. My deepest sympathy to Lydia, who cared for and loved Robyn so deeply. My condolences to all who knew Robyn, this lovely soul. Bye, Robyn."

December 12, 2008 "My sincere condolences to _____ and her family. I would like to offer a special tribute to Lydia whose tireless devotion and compassion made Robyn's brief tenure on this earth one of happiness and love." (Robyn's physician)

"Each life is indeed a gift to be held in our hearts forever. Robyn was indeed a gift to hold in our heart forever. I will never forget her little antics, smiles and loving personality. She was so dear to me and has a special place in my heart." (Robyn's teacher at Victor School)

"Dear Lydia, I loved Robyn. I watched her grow in so many ways. I saw her come out of herself and look around at her world. In the beginning at Victor she was in her own world and it was awesome to watch her start to see the rest of the class. She knew what was going on in the class and quietly peaked out the corner of her eye to keep track of who was doing what. She was quite clever at learning anything that interested her. She knew which object cues to reach for to do her favorite activities such as rest time, music time, switch work and toilet. Who will ever forget her favorite truck wheel toy? She let us know what she did not want to do in her own way. Music and you were her joys in life though. She loved rhythm and could tap out elaborate rhythms with her finger. Even when she was in an unhappy time it was music that calmed her.

You were her other joy Lydia. She would light up for you. She trusted you in the most profound way. There is something very special about you Lydia. I think that Jesus lives in you. You made each person who worked with Robyn feel special and loved. There is nothing quite like a Lydia hug.

I am so sorry that Robyn is no longer with us. I know it was time for her to go and that she was suffering a lot over the last year. I know that she is at peace but I will really miss this dear little girl. I have a picture of her on my bulletin board in the kitchen. She is smiling and looking right into my eyes, that is how I remember her. She has been a joy and a treasure to work with. May God Bless you with love and peace, you and all of Robyn's family will be in my prayers.

Much Love From,

(Robyn's teaching assistant) one of several who worked with Robyn

One of Robyn's many health concerns was chronic urinary tract infections and she had been on many medications in an effort to control these infections. Robyn would sometimes need IV antibiotic treatment to rid her body of the infection. In late 2008 she had a period of relatively good health, without infection and a glowing school report card (November).

It had probably been about 3 years since I had been able to take Robyn for walks in her wheelchair. I used to take her for long walks on the sea walk, stop for lunch or for a coffee, do some shopping and walk back home. We both enjoyed ourselves. Since her health had been deteriorating, her self-abuse escalating we could not go for walks that involved any kind of stopping for breaks. It was okay if you kept walking. Driving was fine too, especially if she had hold of her favourite 'wheel' toy that made noises and sang a tune.

In late 2008 I took Robyn across to the Tillicum Mall on a Saturday and she seemed calm even when the wheelchair stopped for a moment or two. I ordered an Orange Julius and sat down at a table with her beside me in her wheelchair. Robyn just smiled sweetly at me. The tears of joy fell down my cheeks. I had not been able to do that in years. She had only wanted to be in her special veil canopy bed (sometimes tightly swaddled) or out on the road in our special van. We drove by the hour (3-5 hrs) on weekends, sometimes both days of the weekend.

Saturday, November 29 I took Robyn across to the mall for a haircut, she was doing so well. This was something else I had not been able to do because her behaviour had not permitted it. My youngest daughter had agreed to come and stay with Robyn on Sunday because I had been missing so much church in the last months due to Robyn's not feeling well, not wanting to be still in her wheelchair. Robyn sat very still for her haircut and I took the time to enjoy a drink afterward. I brought Robyn home, lowered her into the bathtub, using the Voyageur lift and ceiling track system installed in our home, to get the tiny hairs off her neck and back. While she was relaxing in the tub my daughter and granddaughter arrived. "I will get Robyn out of the tub" my daughter said. A few minutes later I heard "Mom, where is your camera?" "Robyn looks so beautiful!" My daughter took several pictures of Robyn while she was suspended in the sling and then when she was dressed in bed after her bath. I had no idea at the time that those incredibly gorgeous pictures of her were saying goodbye. The next morning my daughter arrived as I was leaving for church. She had planned to take Robyn and her baby, my granddaughter, for a walk while I was at church. I had noticed, earlier Sunday morning, that Robyn was listless, hot with a fever (very unusual for her) so I gave her Tylenol. When I sat her up to dress her, Robyn was limp and whimpered, still hot so I gave her more Tylenol as 4 hours has passed. I started her g-tube feed on the pump and advised my daughter that she should not be going out. When I arrived home from church several hours later I was told that Robyn had hardly stirred and still she was hot. I became alarmed and called the paediatrician on call at the Victoria General Hospital who advised me to bring Robyn in. By Wednesday Robyn was moved from the ward to intensive care and on Saturday, December 6, 2008 she took her last breath.

Lydia's eulogy: Precious Robyn came into our lives in Campbell River almost 13 years ago now. We were praying with mom and dad at the CR Baptist Church, where we attended as families, because things had not gone as expected at her birth. We loved her when we first laid eyes on her in the church nursery. At that time my girls were in grades 8, 10 and 12. My middle daughter was studying at home and I was tutoring from my home. When Robyn was 5 months old we began to look after her in our home from time to time. At the end of 1997 I moved to Victoria with my girls to care for my elderly mother and I also had Robyn about half a month at a time. Before Robyn was 3 years old she was in my care full time. I took on the roll as her foster parent in October 1998.

Now I am looking back at the photos . . . at how quickly the years have gone by . . . people have said to me many times in many settings . . . Lydia, she is so lucky to have you . . . but no, I say, it is I who am so blessed to have her in my life.

I remember many Saturday morning walks into town along the sea walk and across the blue bridge; many more 2 hour plus snuggles in our reclining chair; Robyn's many and varied vocalizations (she loved to hear the sounds she could make and would repeat them incessantly, trading one for the next) One time a lady came to visit and politely asked if I had a pet duck? It was Robyn in her bed.

Robyn's two favourite places, I have to say, were her bed and her van. I loved to just listen to her playing happily in her haven, I mean, bed. Robyn and I have driven and driven and driven some more. We were both restored, refreshed and relaxed on those trips, some lasting as long as 5 hours.

Robyn has introduced me to a world of wonderful people in the medical field: I mention her general physician and her paediatrician; in particular, I know they really cared for her. So many of the nurses at Victoria General Hospital loved her too. There are scores of therapists I would otherwise not have met. Thanks.

Robyn's school, Victor, is one of the best places on this earth and I will miss it so very much—full of truly amazing people—they were like family for Robyn and myself.

My daughter and I were talking with mom a few nights ago about preparing for this day. Mom was saying she had chosen the name Robyn because it means "shining star" and she wanted her life to count and to impact others with the Good News of God's Love. I nearly broke down when I heard this because if I were to share only one thing Robyn taught me that would be it—the real meaning of GOD'S LOVE.

There was a time in my life when I just did not get it. I just did not understand God's love or that it really was for me. I have been a Christian since a very young age and I would even tell you that God loves you and believe it with all my heart but I really did not believe it was for me. One day God said to me . . . . You love this little girl, right? Oh, yes, I do. God said "What can she do to earn your love?" Nothing. "Do you still love her?" Oh, yes. Absolutely. "Does the fact that she can do nothing to earn your love not change the way you feel about her?" No, it has nothing to do with how I feel. "Well, I love her even more than you do" says God. "Can you understand that?" "And I love you too, my daughter. You are precious to me, beautiful and it has nothing to do with what you are doing or are not doing. I just love you." From that moment on I decided to see myself as GOD'S LITTLE ROBYN and whenever I was struggling or doubting God's love for me I just had to be with my little Robyn and be set straight.

We almost lost Robyn in January, 2008 as most of you know and I struggled to let her go then. Family and friends had come to say goodbye. I had peace and had turned her over to the much more capable, safe and gentle arms of Jesus. We have been graced with another 10 months but on Saturday December 6 Robyn told me she had had enough. Her big sister and I were privileged to share the last moment with her.

This is the season when we celebrate the birth of God's Son, Jesus

> **John 3:16 "For God so loved the world that He gave His only begotten Son that whosoever believeth in Him should not perish but have everlasting life."**

Let us remember Robyn at this Christmastime and remember God's gift of love. Thank you mom for trusting me with the care of your precious gift from God. I love you. I miss you Robyn and I will never forget you.

Robyn's memorial service was held on Friday, December 12, 2008. My three daughters, Robyn's foster sisters, took part in the service. My oldest daughter played piano during the service and the eulogy that follows was written by her two sisters, my other daughters.

I am standing up here today because I wanted the chance to share with you a few memories that I will treasure most of Robyn. Before I begin, I would like to read some memories that my sister has written for me to share with you. She writes . . . Almost 13 years ago, in grade 7, I had an English teacher, Robyn's dad, who in my opinion was the most entertaining story teller of all time. It was during that year that His daughter was born, and I had no idea what an impact she would have on our family.

The first time I held her was in the nursery at church—I was alone taking care of her and I rocked her in my arms for half an hour at least, worried with every noise she made that something might be wrong. Little did I know she was as content as could be, just singing away.

Robyn has lived with us for the past 10 years, through thick and thin. Our family broke up, we've moved, we've grown up and changed, gotten married and had babies. Robyn has been with us through it all as our little sister.

There was a time when I felt a little jealous of my mom's devoted attention to Robyn but that didn't last long. I soon realized how much my mom has been blessed by having Robyn in her care. Robyn was my mom's little angel, showing my mom the meaning of unconditional love, and helping her get through some incredibly tough years.

This past summer I took care of Robyn as her intervener for the month of August. It was a challenge, as I also had my 7-month old daughter to care for. Almost every day, I would put my baby in a front carrier and together we would push Robyn in her wheelchair for a couple of hours, which was one of Robyn's favourite things to do. Robyn was sick with C-difficile that month, and it was heartbreaking to watch her suffer so much. She had such a sweet, fun-loving heart with so much potential but was constantly held back by sicknesses.

I choose to believe that Robyn is now in Heaven, with a brand new body and mind like a baby, is exploring the beautiful things about this world and things that we cannot even imagine for the first time. She is having a blast, and one day we will see her again. She will introduce us to her new home.

Love you Robyn, thank you for being such a special part of our lives.

As for my memories, I have always considered myself to be her Big Sister. As sisters usually do, I had a nickname for her, "The Fold Up Doll". She was the most flexible person that I've ever met. She could put her toes up past her head with no troubles. Quite often she would fall asleep completely bent in half at the waist. I loved to watch her sleep. She looked so peaceful.

Her hair is also something that I will remember about her. She could create the most interesting hair-dos. After hours of playing in her bed she would have the biggest bird's nest on the back of her head from having moved her head side to side. Or, if you put a ponytail in her hair, she'd have it half out in no time and hair everywhere. But the sweetest thing that Robyn did with hair was when she was young. She would gently pull my hair and entwine it in her little fingers and try to suck on it. She loved the feeling of hair.

Robyn had a contagious laughter. Sometimes she would laugh and giggle so hard her whole body got going. She'd be lying in bed and laughing for what appeared to be no reason. Obviously something was striking her funny bone. I'd go in and talk to her and ask her what was so funny. She's just laugh even harder. Other times when she'd be coming home from school or an outing she would get so excited in the elevator that she would squeal with delight. When Robyn was feeling well she was full of smiles and happy noises.

What I will miss the most about her is when I'd be visiting at my mom's. I had a habit of going to check on her. Sometimes I'd go all the way in to her room and say hi or sing her goodnight, but other times I'd just stand in the doorway to peek in and see if she was sleeping. I used to love it when I'd go to look in and she would be expecting me. I would see her little head lifted up high, her eyes staring at me through her netted bed. She would have the biggest smile on her face. It was like she was saying to me," I know you're there. You can't sneak up on me. I see you." That is what I will miss the most.

I am so thankful to God that I was able to be there with her for her last moments on this earth. One day soon it will be me saying to her in Heaven, "I see you Robyn!" and we will play together.

One of the songs I sang for Robyn over and over and over again was
You Are My Sunshine. Singing this to her always got a smile even when
Robyn was very sick and in a lot of pain. Family joined me at her graveside in
singing

You are my sunshine, my only sunshine.
You make me happy when skies are grey.
You'll never know dear how much I love you.
Please don't take my sunshine away.

Robyn's uncle put together a DVD tribute to her life for the memorial service.
This music was playing in the background, sung by the African Childrens' Choir.
Robyn loved to listen to their CDs.

For all the times you stood by me, for all the truth that you
made me see.
For all the joy you brought to my life, for all the wrong
that you made right.
For every dream you made come true, for all the love I
found in you.
I'll be forever thankful for you, you're the one who saw me
through.
Through it all.

You were my strength when I was weak.
You were my voice when I couldn't speak.
You were my eyes when I couldn't see.
You saw the best there was in me.
Lifted me up when I couldn't reach.
You gave me faith 'cause you believed.
I'm everything I am because you loved me.

You gave me wings and made me fly.
You touched my hand, I could touch the sky.
I lost my faith, you gave it back to me.
You said no star was out of reach.

I'm everything I am because you loved me.

Chapter VII

REVELATION

Jamaica Road, at the bottom of Mount Douglas and in a 5-bedroom house was where my family and I lived when we left Campbell River at the end of 1997. I am grateful for the nine months my daughters had to be with their grandmother. I know each of my girls treasure their own special memories of her. She did not have a very good appetite anymore, we encouraged her to eat as much as she could of the 'good for her' stuff so she could enjoy what she was really looking forward to—my daughter's homemade chocolate chip cookies. Mom would tell us she was not hungry but her appetite would suddenly re-appear when the cookies arrived. She would actually go on cookie hunts. We would find the Ziploc freezer bags of cookies (frozen) had been cut into with a serrated knife. I guess she could not figure out how to deal with the Ziploc. Cough drops, chocolate chips and bubble gum would mysteriously disappear from around the house as well. I would occasionally find a banana peel or a used tea bag in a baking pan in the cupboard. She had missed the garbage pail. Oh well, I really loved that time with mom. Grandma would ask the blessing for us at dinner:

O Vader die al't leven voedt
Kroon deze tafel met Uw zegen
Spijs en drank ons met het goed
Van Uw milde hand verkregen
Leer ons voor overdaat te wachten
Dat we ons gedragen zoals het behoord
Doe ons het Hemelrijk betrachten
Sterk onzer zielen door Uw Woord.
Amen.

(translation)

Oh Father who takes care of all of life
Crown this table with Your blessing

Nourish us with all the good
We receive from your Hand
Help us not ever to become greedy
And to behave as we should
Cause us to be able to enter eternity
Empower our souls through Your Word.
Amen.

Mom was fascinated with little Robyn who would lie on her back, on the carpet underneath the baby grand piano during my oldest daughter's practise sessions. Robyn became ecstatic with the vibrations, wiggling in time to the music, the louder the better. Sometimes Mom would watch Robyn playing in her walker, sitting in her tumble form or just watch me feeding her. I was able to sublet 2 rooms downstairs. Several very busy months passed. Mom had a fall, hurting her ankle but, due to dementia, she would not keep her pressure bandage on or her leg up on a footstool. My brother, retired from the Navy, already had a job as the administrator at Ebenezer care home in Abbotsford, I was having problems with my landlord across the street so it seemed like the right time to make another move. I spent another 10 months on Cedar Hill X Rd renting a basement before purchasing the condominium in Esquimalt.

My sister and I had talked of living together and possibly opening some kind of group home together some day. We had made a 2-year commitment with each other and the children in our care, where we were renting, and had been looking into possibilities for the future. Robyn was getting heavier, her health concerns more serious at that time. In Esquimalt, because I owned the condominium, I had a ceiling track and lift system installed. It allowed me to take Robyn from her bed to the bathtub across the hall. In View Royal, where we were now renting, our landlord would not allow the installation of the ceiling track and lift system. Fortunately, I was able to have Robyn's special bed taken apart and re-assembled at our new location. I remember a 5-month period while living in that rancher when Robyn could not go to school. She was in so much pain because of undetected kidney stones that she was tightly wrapped in flannel sheets, looking like a burrito and still she thrashed about in bed like a bucking bronco. The floor would vibrate because of her movements and my heart was breaking. She would not sit in her wheelchair. Much of the time I could not even hold her. Robyn did get her much needed surgery on a Friday in the spring of 2004. She was taken to hospital by ambulance. I instructed the paramedics with respect to her self-abusive behaviour relative to pain, and how she needed to be wrapped for security and comfort. I followed the ambulance with our van and wheelchair, making the 3-minute drive to the hospital. When I arrived I saw the attendant holding Robyn who had come out of her wrap and the attendant was in tears. He could not stand to see the suffering. Her physician was in attendance and he told me the procedure done by her paediatric urologist took less than 3 minutes. I drove her home a couple of days later, in her wheelchair, sitting behind me in her van with a smile on her face. She was back in school on Monday. At our follow-up appointment the urologist was quick to apologize to me and promised that he would listen to me if there were a next time. Robyn had already had kidney stones removed 4 years prior to this event and I had been pleading with him to intervene. The nephrologist that had helped Robyn in 2000 was no longer practising in Victoria. I knew that a move had to be made at the end of our 2-year commitment in View Royal. My sister and I had done some looking at houses and were even thinking of moving to Sooke, our old stomping grounds, but we knew it really was too far away from the amenities needed for the care of the special needs children, Robyn especially.

January,2005, brought an unexpected turn of events into our lives. My middle daughter, almost 24 years old, a student at Camosun College studying accounting, collapsed in the stairwell while on a break. Following the break she was to give a presentation to the class. I got a call from her younger sister to come to the hospital where she had been taken by ambulance. Apparently she had had a seizure. When I arrived at the hospital I was told she had a second seizure at the hospital—the definition of epilepsy. My daughter came to stay with me during the daytime for a while in order to adjust to this new frightening reality in her life. My sister, unfortunately, was unable to cope with the additional strain that this unexpected family crisis added to our living situation in the 2-bedroom rancher. After 2 ½ weeks she let me know that she felt our place was too small for this kind of living and if it continued she and her special needs child would look for another place to live. I was very upset by her words. Our 2-year commitment would not be finished until April. This was my daughter who really needed me at a very difficult time in her life. I remembered what my sister had said to me earlier, when she came to live with me in Esquimalt, that she had no idea I was still so enmeshed in my children's lives. I could not understand this. I went out for a 2-hour drive, I prayed and cried out to God. I went back and spoke to my sister. I told her that she could go if she felt she needed to go but that I would not live anywhere that one of my children were not welcome. My sister did get a place of her own by March and by June or July she returned to the East Coast. That is how I ended up buying, through God's provision, another condominium. Robyn and I shared accommodations again and re-installed the ceiling track and lift system. I was so very hurt, angry and disillusioned at that time in my life. I felt that I had given up so much for my sister.

It was not easy to start over, on my own in many respects but, I knew that God was with me and He had brought me to this place, this building, for a reason. I had my hands full just settling in, adjusting to all the newness. I had been in the building in Esquimalt for 3 ½ years, becoming comfortable with several of my neighbours. I sat on Council as President before selling. My new building was certainly different. I couldn't put my finger on it at first but I sensed that things were not running smoothly here. We have a Resident Caretaker in the building and in my first 5 months here, there was a turnover of 3 caretakers. Being an owner, I knew there would be Strata Council and a Property Management company but what I did not know was that there was also a large Rent Pool in the building. Interesting dynamics. My Esquimalt building had a 1% rental allowance. I had no intentions of becoming involved here but when the third caretaker, a pleasant fellow, explained he was let go for no apparent reason, I decided it was time for me to go to a meeting and let my voice be heard. To make what could be a long story, short, I began to see that communication between Council, Property Management and Caretaker was not good at all. In April 2009 I began my second year as President of the Strata Council in this building, things have changed for the better. The caretaker and I work wonderfully well together.

Back to that first winter on my own with Robyn, in my new place, I remember struggling with the old feelings of depression, loneliness and isolation. I had gone off antidepressants, however, and was determined to stay off. My oldest daughter invited me to an early December, Friday evening, Ladies', Christmas tea at her church. I had received a call, rather voicemail, earlier in the week from a lady friend at Oaklands Chapel offering to pick me up and take me for coffee on the following Saturday. I remember having to force myself to say yes to both of these invitations because of the strong urge to keep to myself, stop reaching out as I had been let down and disappointed so much already. My daughter picked me up for the tea and we have a very nice time. While I was getting out of her car at home she told me that she was concerned about me and wondered if I shouldn't be seeing a counsellor. I knew that my daughter was demonstrating her love for me and it would have taken courage for her to advise me this way. The next morning my lady friend picked me up and took me out for breakfast and we had a very nice visit. To my amazement and in answer to my prayers, when she dropped me off, she offered to have me come to her home for counselling. It would cost me nothing. I had such a desperate need for connection, friendship and relationship at that time in my life and this was a wonderful answer. I had several sessions over a period of months with my counsellor friend and these were times of great blessing, growth, prayer and healing in my life.

I travelled with Robyn if she needed to be seen by a specialist on the mainland in Vancouver, for instance. In the summer we would spend a week at a special camp for other children like Robyn who were classed as deafblind, their parents, siblings and the children's intervenors, which was also on the mainland. Several times each year Robyn would get respite at Sunnyhill Health Centre for Children in Vancouver for a period of 5 or 6 days. While she was there I would stay with my brother and sister-in-law who live in Abbotsford, having a wonderful time relaxing with them. I remember one time when my counsellor had given me an assignment. I was to ask my brother questions about our family dynamics and how things had been from his perspective. We had a most interesting discussion. I wondered if we really were part of the same family. Perspective is a wonderful thing. I love my brother and sister-in-law so very much, we have shared deeply and I know there is more to come. On my own I had picked up materials and studied on learning to listen to the voice of God. This was something else that I discovered I could share with my sister-in-law as she too had been reading and studying on this topic. She and I have shared a special relationship for many years already. As I was making my way through a workbook I began to realize that I had heard God's voice but it just was not as much in the forefront of my awareness as I would like it to be.

Forgiveness and reconciliation, although it was definitely a lengthy process, between my sister and I, has occurred, Praise God. I had already learned of the importance of forgiveness and reconciliation in significant relationships and would not allow anything to hold me back from all that God has for me in this life. I remember the day I walked out of my principal's office in Campbell River after making an appointment with him to tell him that I forgave him for any wrongs he had committed towards me in the process of letting me go. I did not want there to be a root of bitterness taking hold in my heart. I walked out of that office as if on air because I had been obedient to the prompting of the Holy Spirit. I remember too, my deliverance experience with the DWJD ministry. I had forgiven my husband, obtained a divorce and had very little contact with him. He would call me only if he needed to be in touch with one of our daughters and had been unable to reach them. During those calls I found myself inevitably uncomfortable for no reason apparent to me. At the time of my deliverance it was explained to me that soul ties needed to be broken and they were. God had my ex-husband call the day after I arrived home from the deliverance ministry meeting to confirm for me my glorious deliverance. For the first time since leaving Campbell River at the end of 1997, his call had no affect on me whatsoever, and no calls from him have affected me in a negative way since my deliverance. Praise God.

Learning to listen to God's voice became a delight for me. My relationship with God improved as I became more consistent with my devotional times of Bible reading and prayer and practised listening for His voice. When I considered Robyn's health concerns, as well as my own for that matter, I wondered how much longer I would be able to look after her. I took a course in medical terminology on-line as well as medical transcription with a view to a change of occupation should something happen to Robyn or myself. I completed the medical terminology course while the transcription course is ongoing. 2008 was a difficult year with respect to Robyn's health as was mentioned in her chapter. There were many trips to the hospital by ambulance. Life was stressful. I would have hot baths when I could, in the early mornings and to my pleasure and surprise, that is when God would speak to me. I could hear Him. It was absolutely delightful to me. Perhaps that is when and where He could best get my attention because I would let go a little and relax. I do not know for sure but I do know for sure that often, when I am in the tub, He speaks to me and I love it.

Another source of great healing and blessing in my life was the revelation, my coming to understand the meaning of Galatians 3:13-14 "Christ hath redeemed us from the curse of the law, being made a curse for us: for it is written, Cursed is every one that hangeth on a tree: That the blessing of Abraham might come on the Gentiles through Jesus Christ; that we might receive the promise of the Spirit through faith." I studied Derek Prince's book, Blessing or Curse and appropriated the truths explained therein.

In 2008 I had also begun to keep a spiritual journal to have a record of the things God was showing me through His word. I was attending Bible study and prayer meetings more regularly again at Victory Chapel. My pastor would meet with me once in 6 weeks or so to go through my journal with me. This had started because when I was learning to listen to God's voice, the workbook suggestion was to invite a mentor to check on my journaling and get an experienced opinion as to whether or not it was the voice of God I was hearing. I love my pastor. We still meet one on one occasionally to go through my spiritual journal and have such a sweet time of fellowship. I remember as a 9-year old girl writing in my school journal that I was going to Africa to be a missionary when I grew up. I believe that now, God has brought Africa to me. I have filled two 100-page notebooks since I began journaling in 2008 but I will include only the page I titled God's love letter to me, February 24, 2009. (From Psalm 31)

O Lord, I have come to you for protection; don't let me be disgraced. Save me, for you do what is right. Turn your ear to

listen to me; rescue me quickly. Be my rock of protection, a fortress where I will be safe. You are my rock and my fortress. For the honor of your name, lead me out of this danger. Pull me from the trap my enemies set for me, for I find protection in you alone. I entrust my spirit into your hand. Rescue me, Lord, for you are a faithful God . . . . I will be glad and rejoice in your unfailing love, for you have seen my troubles, and you care about the anguish of my soul. You have not handed me over to my enemies but have set me in a safe place. Have mercy on me, Lord, for I am in distress. Tears blur my eyes. My body and soul are withering away. I am dying from grief; my years are shortened by sadness . . . But I am trusting you, O Lord, saying, You are my God. My future is in your hands . . . . Let your favor shine on your servant. In your unfailing love, rescue me. Don't let me be disgraced, O Lord, for I call out to you for help. Let the wicked be disgraced; let them lie silent in the grave. Silence their lying lips—those proud and arrogant lips that accuse the godly. How great is the goodness you have stored up for those who fear you. You lavish it on those who come to you for protection, blessing them before the watching world. You hide them in the shelter of your presence, safe from those who conspire against them. You shelter them in your presence, far from accusing tongues. Praise the Lord, for he has shown me the wonders of his unfailing love. He kept me safe when my city was under attack . . . . So be strong and courageous, all you who put your hope in the Lord.

This passage of scripture came at a time in my life when I needed it most. I was grieving Robyn's passing, had lost my income, needed to look for a new job and needed to sell the lift-equipped van. Because I had completed the medical terminology course, was still working on the transcription I decided to try and find work with the Vancouver Island Health Authority as a clerk. The application process began in February 2009.

My oldest daughter has been married for 6 years. She and her husband have a beautiful 6-year old daughter and she has a 4-year old brother. October 2007, on my birthday, my second daughter was married. The following month my youngest daughter was married and in January 2008 her daughter was born, my third grandchild.

My oldest daughter and her family live in Victoria, which delights me. My second daughter is an amazing woman of faith who is no stranger to struggles in her life. She has had to endure the addition of the diagnosis of lupus to her condition of epilepsy and is on a constant regimen of medicines. After only 1½ years of marriage she and her husband find themselves separated by reason of his need for a recovery program. My daughter is a hard worker, not a quitter, I have a great deal of admiration for her passion for Jesus and her love for her husband. She knows how to stand by her man.

My youngest married an Australian who was living and working in Canada for a year before they said goodbye. We celebrated their daughter's first birthday together, the month before they were gone, we miss them terribly. I am thankful for Facebook, however, as it allows me the opportunity to keep in touch with this family, to see pictures and to hear updates. Before leaving Canada, this daughter kindly re-painted my bathroom and bedroom. She wanted me to have fresh start and room of my own. I had always shared my bedroom with Robyn. Now there was a memorial for her in the living room.

February, March and April I was applying and re-applying for those VIHA positions. My van wasn't selling. The economy was bad. I cried out to God one night in my bed in desperation and pleading Psalm 31, reminding Him that I was counting on his favour to shine on me. The next day I got a call for an interview. I was so excited. I had been applying for positions as a Unit Clerk because of the transcription course I was taking, but I learned in my interview that I did not qualify as a Unit Clerk. I needed to apply for positions as a Clerk and to register for the course to become a Unit Clerk. That has been taken care of. I am still excited about the way God answers prayer. That interview was wonderful. The Nurse Manager told me I would be an excellent candidate for the position, she was very impressed with my resume. I have been applying for Clerk positions without response ever since. Near the middle of March I decided to take the van to Chilliwack where it had been purchased in 2007. I felt that prospective buyers would be inclined to frequent this place of business, I did not want to put more mileage on the vehicle and Robyn was no longer riding behind me in her wheelchair. I had made up my mind. A friend at my church offered me the use of one of her vehicles for a few weeks until mine sold. She would need her vehicle back as she was making a trip at the end of April. What a wonderful blessing that was, Praise God.

Pastor told us at church that the Redeemed Christian Church of God had declared the year 2009 to be the year of the supernatural. I began to pray that I would understand what it meant to walk by faith and not by sight, to live as though I really believed God's Word. My devotional times were becoming more precious and meaningful by the day. I had experienced power to overcome

---

despair in praising God, it is scriptural that God inhabits the praises of His people. God's timing is always perfect. My friend needed her vehicle back, I returned it in advance of the deadline. Our pastor had been given a vehicle. He gifted me with the van he would no longer be using. Praise God. It needed some mechanical repairs but has been running well since those have been done. I was making payments on the 2006 van,which had not sold yet, still looking for work and my funds were all but exhausted. I chose to hang on and to keep on trusting. My second daughter and I had talked about moving in together since Robyn had passed away, her husband was not at home and I was in a position to be able to offer my condo for rent. We both prayed about this for some time and then agreed that it would be a good thing for us to do. I advertised my place for the first of June, actually started sleeping upstairs at my daughter's by the middle of May and was completely moved in before the end of the month. Nearing the end of the month, one day when I was downstairs checking telephone messages I picked up a call from Chilliwack informing me of some good news. My van had sold. Praise God. His timing is perfect. No more van payments. I was now able to pay out the van loan as well as some other bills.

This year has been one of incredible growth and learning for me, in the things of the supernatural realm, in particular. I have established the habit of taking notes at church because of the richness of pastor's messages. I want to take it all in and reflect on the words throughout the week. Sometime in April God spoke to me and told me that he wanted me to write a book. I was astounded at this. I never dreamed that this would be asked of me. I cannot remember having a desire to be an author. I know that I have a desire to be obedient and to trust my LORD and my SAVIOUR. I began to gather notes here and there as I felt inspired, or led by the Spirit. Often words or thoughts would come as I was having my devotional time or when I was in the bathtub. I was surprised one Sunday when I was taking notes on the message and God said to me, in my spirit, "this is for the book" I had to keep a separate column as God brought things to my recollection that He wanted me to include in my writing. I learned to keep a pad and pen everywhere, including by the tub because I never knew when the inspiration might come or the flow would be turned on. From the time God first asked me to write until now has only been 3 months. One of those months,things came to a halt, so to speak, because of my move from the third to fourth floor in my building. I have been seriously writing for less than 3 weeks. God is doing this work through me. I chose to trust and obey. Up until now my life has had so many unanswered questions but now, my life makes sense. If God had provided a job for me before now, I would not have been able to do this writing and had this incredible experience. My life has become a message, my privilege to share with God's blessing.

—

Two mornings ago, so close to finishing my manuscript my computer crashed. I know who my enemy is and he was promptly rebuked. In a matter of seconds the situation was resolved and I was able to carry on. Praise God. I knew that the enemy we wrestle with would have to be contended with because this message is important and he does not want it to get out there but it will get out there. The battle is already won in Jesus name.

Isaiah 55:10-11 "For as the rain cometh down, And the snow from heaven, And returneth not thither, But watereth the earth, And maketh it bring forth and bud, That it may give seed to the sower, and bread to the eater: So shall my word be that goeth forth out of my mouth: It shall not return unto me void, But it shall accomplish that which I please, And it shall prosper in the thing whereto I sent it."

He wraps himself in Light, and darkness tries to hide
And trembles at His voice, Trembles at His voice

How great is our God, sing with me how great is our God
And all will see how great, how great is our God

Age to age He stands and time is in His hands
Beginning and the end, beginning and the end

The Godhead Three in One, Father Spirit Son
The Lion and the Lamb, the Lion and the Lamb

Name above all names, worthy of all praise
My heart will sing how great is our God

Have you read the papers, do you hear what they say?
Rising unemployment, cost of living every day is getting higher
Another suicide bomber in a bus with 13 kids it kind of makes me wonder
What those children ever did
Yet we still go to church and sing shout to the LORD
And we lift Holy hands and we're reading His Word
Now I'm sitting by my piano with nothing to play
But that doesn't change the fact that God is God anyway.
So I sing bless ye the LORD through my trials and all my troubles
I have come with a heart of worship.
For the gift of your Son for the grace to fight my battles
I have come to you with thanksgiving.

—

Hear my humble cry. See my broken spirit but
In every situation I'll still choose to worship you.

Please forgive me this is not your normal worship song.
I tried to write a simple song that me and everyone could sing along but
I realized that there is something about praise it shouldn't only come
When all is seemingly okay
So when you start to cry like your life is a mess don't be scared,
Don't be discouraged, it is only a test.
Why don't you lift up your voice to the ears of your God and
Release sweet smelling savour from your alabaster box
Singing bless ye the LORD through my trials and all my troubles
I have come with a heart of worship
For the gift of your Son, for the grace to fight my battles
I have come to you with thanksgiving.
Though the flowers die, see the branches wither but
When the troubles multiply I'll still choose to worship You.

I worship You Almighty God. There is none like You.
Jesus lover of my soul.
Highly exalted one to whom all praise is due.

www.ingramcontent.com/pod-product-compliance
Lightning Source LLC
Chambersburg PA
CBHW021248280526
45784CB00005B/2278